REVERSE
Live Differently

STUDENT DEVOTIONAL

Greg Stier

DARE 2 SHARE

Reverse

Copyright © 2014 Dare 2 Share Ministries.
All rights reserved.

A D2S Publishing book
PO Box 745323
Arvada, CO 80006

All scripture quotations, unless otherwise indicated, are taken from the *Holy Bible*, New Living Translation, copyright © 1996, 2004, 2007 by Tyndale House Foundation. Used by permission of Tyndale House Publishers, Inc., Carol Stream, Illinois 60188. All rights reserved.

Scripture quotations marked (NIV) are taken from the *Holy Bible*, New International Version®, NIV®. Copyright © 1973, 1978, 1984 by Biblica, Inc™ Used by permission of Zondervan. All rights reserved worldwide.

No part of this publication may be reproduced, stored in a retrieval system, or transmitted in any form or by any means—electronic, mechanical, photocopy, recording, or otherwise—without prior permission of the publisher.

Stier, Greg
Reverse: live differently
ISBN: 978-0-9725507-0-3
Library of Congress Control Number: 2013945832
Printed in the United States of America
1 2 3 4 5 6 7 8 9 / 14 13 12 11 10 09 08

Dedication

To every teenager who's ever strived and struggled to live with a God-focus in a me-focused world.

Table of Contents

Яeverse Living...v

Week One: Relate Differently

Daniel: God's Man with a Mission 1

We're Not in Kansas Anymore.. 5

Cool in a Crisis 9

Wisdom and Influence 13

All-Encompassing Compassion 17

A God in Heaven 21

Big Dreams 25

Week Two: Think Differently

Idols Then and Now.. 29

Jealousy Unleashed 33

A Lethal Line in the Sand 37

How to Grow a Backbone 41

PU – Persecution University 45

Rescue!.. 49

Limb from Limb 53

Week Three: Act Differently

Pursue Excellence 57

Live with Integrity.. 61

Bold & Brave... 65

Pray, Pray, Pray, Three Times a Day 69

Facing the Darkest Night... 73

Total Trust... 77

The God Who Rescues 81

Яeverse Living:
Intense, Deep, Vibrant, Risky, Rewarding, Immense

Just look at the world around you and at the secret interior life inside you and you'll see it's true: life can get intense. Relationally intense, in terms of how you interact with others. Inside-your-head intense as you think about and process things. How-to-live-your-life intense when it comes to your choices and actions.

But in the midst of the intensity of life, God has plans for you. In fact, He has BIG plans for you—He longs for a deep, rich, vibrant relationship between you and Him, and He is calling you to the most important job on the planet, bringing His hope and truth to those around you.

In a nutshell, you could summarize His desires for you like this: To know Him and make Him known.

God's desires for you as His follower stand in dramatic opposition to how the world around you is living life. Our world is largely me-focused, rather than God-focused. That's why I call living with a God-focus living in "reverse." It's a totally different way to live—deep, wild, intense, exciting, risky and immensely satisfying—because it's living in tune with the way God designed us to live, in relationship with Him.

We see this kind of reverse living on full display in one of my favorite Old Testament books of the Bible: Daniel. Daniel and his friends were totally tuned into the one, true God they loved, trusted and served. And because of that God-focus, they related differently, thought differently and acted differently than the world around them. While still teenagers, they exhibited immense courage as they were swept up in the ravages of war. And as they continued to keep their focus on God, they lived godly lives of excellence and integrity; lives that changed the course of history across kingdoms and centuries.

In these next three weeks of daily devos, we'll be looking at three themes from three compelling, courageous stories out of the book of Daniel.

Week 1: **Relate Differently.** Daniel's interpretation of the king's dream (Daniel 2)

Week 2: **Think Differently.** Shadrach, Meshach, and Abednego in the fiery furnace (Daniel 3)

Week 3: **Act Differently.** Daniel in the lion's den (Daniel 6)

Each of these stories gives us a brutally honest window into what bravely living in reverse looked liked for Daniel & Co. as they sought to know God and make Him known, facing down extreme danger and persecution while their very lives hung in the balance.

But these three stories are more than interesting, entertaining reading. They provide amazingly powerful, relevant insights for you as you seek to live in reverse today in the very place God has planted you—in the midst of the good, the bad and the ugly intensity of life right now.

Of course, living in reverse will look distinctly different in each person's life. How you personally live it out will be as unique as your fingerprints, your personality, your passions and your circumstances. That's why this devo is packed full of opportunities for you to apply what you're learning personally, day by day. Here's a quick roadmap of how the typical devo is structured:

Яead – Identifies the Bible passage for the day.

Яecharge – Provides some context and a brief recap of the Bible passage.

Яeflect – Unpacks how the timeless truth found in the passage is relevant to you personally.

Яeverse – Presents a concrete, personal application that challenges you to live in reverse.

Яemember – Recommends a tool or tip to help you share Jesus' message with others.

Яenew – Provides a guided prayer as you seek God's help in applying what you've learned (if the devo for the day doesn't already include a prayer time).

As you explore these three stories in the book of Daniel, you'll discover some invaluable, timeless truths. Let them ignite your walk with God and transform you into a Jesus follower who, like Daniel, can rock your world and change the course of history for all eternity!

#1 DANIEL: GOD'S MAN WITH A MISSION

Яecharge

Besieged, beaten and destined for bondage. Daniel found himself swept up in a defeat of catastrophic proportions. Along with many of his Jewish countrymen, he was taken captive by the conquering Babylonian army in 605 B.C, while he was still a teenager.

Sucked into the upheaval of war, and hauled off to Babylon to become a servant to his new master, King Nebuchadnezzar, Daniel could have easily seen himself as just a young, helpless pawn in a power struggle between nations. But Daniel refused to wallow in distress and despair. The trials he faced were not a wedge that drove him away from God; instead, the Book of Daniel gives us a striking look into how his trials served as a wedge that pushed him even closer to God.

Daniel put his trust in the Almighty God who had uprooted him from his old life and transplanted him to a new one. He displayed an unshakeable confidence that God was large and in charge. He was a young man with a mission and a message: to know God and make Him known.

The Book of Daniel is a mix of Daniel's personal story and his prophecies foretelling some critical aspects of God's unfolding plan across the sweep of history. Daniel's personal story is packed with exciting, dramatic incidents—like Daniel in the lion's den, and his three friends' heated encounter with a fiery furnace. But his prophecies are equally exciting and dramatic. They predicted four of the coming earthly kingdoms whose rise and fall would directly impact the nation of Israel, and also describe the coming eternal, heavenly kingdom to be established by Jesus the Messiah.

Яeflect

The Bible tells us that life works best when it's lived out of a deep, intimate relationship with God. A give-and-take relationship that's so vibrant and powerful that it will carry you through thick and thin. God wants this kind of relationship with you so He can meet you in the midst of both the joy and the pain—no matter what. Even when life seems unfair or grows uncomfortable, He will walk beside you through it all as you connect with Him at that deep, personal level. He did that for Daniel, and He'll do it for you.

And you have something else in common with Daniel. No matter who you are or where you live, God has a mission and message for you too: to know Him and make Him known. Now it's time to unpack some of what that looks like...

Яeverse

Right now, in the midst of whatever's going on in your life—good, bad or ugly, does God feel distant or close to you? Take a few minutes to write a note to God about how you're feeling. Then ask Him to help you go deeper with Him in the coming days.

DEAR GOD,

LATELY I'VE BEEN FEELING LIKE YOU AND I ARE...

_____

_____

_____

_____

_____

_____

_____

_____

_____

_____

_____

_____

_____

_____

_____

Яemember

Everyone is going through stuff. Think about a non-Christian friend
who is stressed or struggling right now. Pray that you can find a way
to encourage them today.

Яenew

Father, I pray that in the days ahead You will help me learn how
to connect with You on a deeper, more intimate level. I want a
relationship with You that will carry me through good times and bad.
Show me what living in reverse looks like for me, and give me the
courage to live differently. In Jesus' name, amen.

#2 WE'RE NOT IN KANSAS ANYMORE

Яead
Daniel 2:1-11

Яecharge
Snagged as the "spoils of war" and whisked
away to Babylon's foreign culture, Daniel and some of
the other smart, physically fit Hebrew teenagers were pulled
aside for special treatment. For three years the King's court officials
immersed these promising young men in a new way of thinking and
trained them for the position of "wise men" in the royal court.

Daniel and his friends found themselves transported from their
devout Hebrew roots into a swirling marketplace of spiritual ideas.
They routinely rubbed shoulders with the king's other "wise men"—

described as "astrologers, enchanters, magicians and sorcerers"—whose jobs included interpreting the king's dreams using their "dark arts."

Now, their "dark arts" were failing to deliver what the king demanded: an explanation for his troubling dream. Their false, empty promises were being uncloaked as the spiritual imposters they'd been all along.

Яeflect

Can you relate to Daniel's situation? While you probably don't have "astrologers, enchanters, magicians and sorcerers" sitting across the aisle from you in class, you do face a swirling marketplace of spiritual influences and worldviews. YouTube, music, movies, porn, friends, enemies, TV, parties…you're surrounded by a wide range of cultural inputs trying to influence you in ways that pull you away from God. You're bombarded by mind-shifting messages about things like beauty, stuff, success and sex.

It can be a real struggle to keep your focus on God in the midst of all of this.

Яeverse

How are you doing at discerning God's truth and exposing the false, empty promises clamoring for your soul? Ask God to help you hear His voice of truth, as you dive deep into His Word. Take a few minutes and jot down some thoughts about how you're doing. Here are a couple areas to consider…

APPEARANCE. The culture tells me I'm more valuable if I'm attractive and have cool clothes. But God, you tell me, *"Don't be concerned about the outward beauty of fancy hairstyles, expensive jewelry, or beautiful clothes. You should clothe yourselves instead with the beauty that comes from within, the unfading beauty of a gentle and quiet spirit, which is so precious to God"* (1 Peter 3:3-4).

_____

_____

_____

_____

STUFF. The culture tells me to want more toys, more tech, more money, more stuff. But Jesus, you tell me, *"Wherever your treasure is, there the desires of your heart will also be "* (Matthew 6:21).

_____

_____

_____

_____

Яemember

Do you have friends who are trapped in the emptiness of a life lived apart from God's truth? Start praying for them. Ask God to begin working in their hearts and lives to prepare them to hear Jesus' message of hope and truth.

Яenew

Father, help me hear Your truth from Your Word and stay focused on You. Expose the false, empty promises the world around me tries to get me to buy into. In Jesus' name, amen.

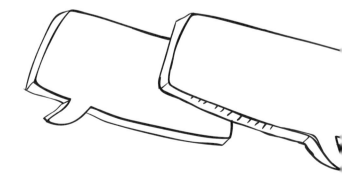

#3 COOL IN A CRISIS

Яead
Daniel 2:12-19

Яecharge
They were all going to die!

The king was so outraged by his wise men's failure to interpret his troubling dream, that he issued a blanket death sentence for all of them—including Daniel and his three friends. But even in a deadly crisis, Daniel kept his wits about him. He was not thrown into panic or despair.

Not at all. Daniel's faith in God kept hope alive. Instead of fruitless protest or effusive excuses, Daniel asked the relevant questions that would give him a pulse on the full situation, then quickly became a young man with a plan, intent on rescuing all of them from death.

Daniel approached the king and asked for more time, exuding a confidence that the dream could be interpreted—a confidence born out of his steadfast faith that his God was large and in charge. Then, once the king's temporary stay of execution was secured, Daniel laid the critical groundwork every crisis calls for: PRAYER. He immediately enlisted his three Hebrew friends, Hananiah, Mishael and Azariah, to pray and plead for God's mercy concerning the king's mysterious dream. (FYI, the Babylonians changed these guys' names to Shadrach, Meshach and Abednego.)

And during the night, their prayers were answered. God revealed the king's dream to Daniel in a vision.

Яeflect

How about you? When the going gets tough, is your first instinct to run away, when instead you should lean on God and enlist your Christian friends to rally round you with prayer and encouragement?

While you might not be facing down a literal life-and-death situation like Daniel was, all of us confront tough stuff in our lives: broken relationships, painful rejections, stress, family conflicts, the loss of a loved one and shattered dreams, to name a few.

When you find yourself facing discouragement or distress, don't run, and don't try to stand alone. Develop a plan for dealing with it, rally some friends and lean in to these three incredible resources: your faith in God, prayer and your Christian friends. Here are some truths from God's Word that you can cling to:

> *"So be strong and courageous! Do not be afraid and do not panic before them. For the Lord your God will personally go ahead of you. He will neither fail you nor abandon you"* (Deuteronomy 31:6).

Don't worry about anything; instead, pray about everything. Tell God what you need, and thank him for all he has done (Philippians 4:6).

If you've never experienced the kind of loving, personal relationship with God described in the passages above, I invite you to enter into that kind of relationship now by trusting in Jesus for your salvation. Check out the GOSPEL box at the end of today's devo entry to learn about this free gift of grace.

Яeverse
Is there some stressor that's causing discouragement or difficulty in your life, or in the life of someone you care about? Start praying about it today. Ask a few friends to begin praying with you. Seek advice from godly Christians you respect (both peers and adults) so they can help you maneuver your way through the tough stuff.

Яemember
Daniel developed a plan to rescue himself and his friends. Go to www.dare2share.org/thecause/the-cause-circle/ for a simple tool to help you become more purposeful in your efforts to reach and rescue your friends who need Jesus.

Яenew
Dear God, thank You that I can run to You when things get tough. Thank You that You always understand me and that I can bring all my requests and concerns to You. In Jesus' name, amen.

THE GOSPEL

The word gospel means "good news," and is explained by the following six key truths.

G od created us to be with Him. (Genesis 1-2)
O ur sins separate us from God. (Genesis 3)
S ins cannot be removed by good deeds. (Genesis 4 – Malachi 4)
P aying the price for sin, Jesus died and rose again. (Matthew – Luke)
E veryone who trusts in Him alone has eternal life. (John)
L ife with Jesus starts now and lasts forever. (Acts - Revelation)

Is there anything holding you back from putting your faith in Jesus right now to give you eternal life? The moment you trust in Jesus, you enter into an eternal relationship with God. Your life will never be the same. Both now and forever.

While saying a prayer isn't what gets you into a relationship with God, it is a way for you to express your newfound faith in Jesus. You might pray something like this...

"Dear God, I know that my sins have broken my relationship with You, and that nothing I could do could ever change that. But right now, I believe that Jesus died in my place and rose again from the dead. I trust in Him to forgive me for my sins. Through faith in Him, I am entering an eternal relationship with You. Thank You for this free gift! Amen."

For more information, go to www.LifeIn6Words.com.

#4 WISDOM AND INFLUENCE

Яead
Daniel 2: 20-23

Яecharge
Daniel knew without a doubt that God was the source of the wisdom he'd received to interpret the king's dream, and the giver of the influential position he had at the king's court. You hear it clearly in this line of Daniel's prayer: *"I thank and praise you, God of my ancestors: You have given me wisdom and power, you have made known to me what we asked of you"* (Daniel 2:23. NIV).

But something even bigger was about to happen here. Not only was God supernaturally intervening to save these doomed young men's lives, He was also bringing together the pieces of the puzzle that was Daniel's life. The tragic, traumatic twists and turns of being a captive of the Babylonians were being redeemed through God's unfolding larger plan and purpose.

God was about to use Daniel to carry His message to King Nebuchadnezzar.

Яeflect

God has a larger plan and purpose for your life, too: to know Him and make Him known. It's not just super-prophets like Daniel who God wants to use as His message-bearers. It's you too! That's what Jesus meant when He told His followers in Acts 1:8, *"You will be my witnesses, telling people about me everywhere."*

God's intent is that you be the bearer of His gospel message where you live. Whether it's your friends from school, sports, work or whatever, you can carry Jesus' message of hope to them. God will provide you with wisdom and influence, too. In fact, James 1:5-6 says godly wisdom is ours for the asking:

> *If you need wisdom, ask our generous God, and he will give it to you. He will not rebuke you for asking. But when you ask him, be sure that your faith is in God alone. Do not waver, for a person with divided loyalty is as unsettled as a wave of the sea that is blown and tossed by the wind.*

And you already have far more personal influence than you probably realize. It's actually been demonstrated in a social media study that, as a friend, you have 100 times more influence on your own friends than a stranger does. That means YOU are the best person to talk to your friends who don't know about Jesus or the gospel!

Яeverse

God has promised you His wisdom and specifically placed you in your own sphere of influence. Spend some time asking Him for the wisdom you need to reach your friends with His message.

DEAR GOD,
I'M ASKING YOU FOR WISDOM BECAUSE...

_____

_____

_____

_____

_____

I WANT TO INFLUENCE MY FRIENDS
and nudge them closer to You because...

_____

_____

_____

_____

Яemember

Get the training and tools you need to help you be wise about sharing Jesus' message of hope. Check out www.dare2share.org/worldviews for specific, practical training and ideas about how to have deeper spiritual conversations with your friends.

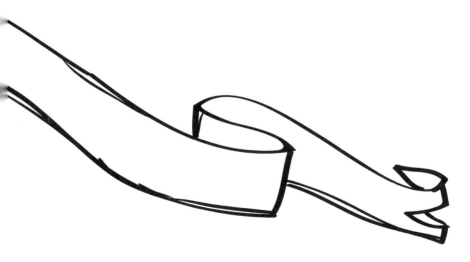

#5 ALL-ENCOMPASSING COMPASSION

Яead
Daniel 2:24

Яecharge
Now that Daniel had the inside scoop about the king's dream, he needed to save his neck. So he hurried to the king's executioner, Arioch.

You might have expected him to say something like this: "Ari, my man, me and my three friends, Shad, Mesh and Abs, we pulled an all-nighter and applied all our brilliance and brain power to this seriously deep dilemma. We've figured it out, man! So first things first, make sure the four of us are off your kill list, then take me to the king…"

But Daniel 2:24 shows us a strikingly different picture. Daniel chose to leverage the knowledge he'd been given and include **all** the king's wise men in his request that the king's executioner stand down. He wanted to rescue not just his own inner circle of friends, but also the "competition," even those entangled in the dark arts of sorcery. Daniel's compassion extended beyond his buddies to the lost—the clueless, the deluded and even the hostile.

Яeflect

How far does your compassion reach?

It can be easy to camp in the safety and comfort of your own little clique. It's easy to hold grudges or just plain write people off as too far beyond God's reach, thinking "They're so hostile to God…" or "They're so into that really dark stuff…"

Daniel was dealing with **Babylonians,** after all, the guys who were holding him and the other Hebrews **captive**. Yet he extended compassion to this crowd, and intervened to save their lives.

Our human hearts sometimes seem to be on some sort of bad auto-pilot setting when it comes to rejecting or tormenting those who are "different" from us. From our country's history of slavery and discrimination, to today's sex slaves in Thailand, to the Holocaust, to the bullying that goes on at your school, we humans are experts on looking out for our own interests, all the while ignoring the desperate plight of others who are "different."

Daniel didn't buy into this attitude. And Jesus didn't either. Listen to His words in Matthew 5:44-47:

But I say, love your enemies! Pray for those who persecute you! In that way, you will be acting as true children of your Father in heaven. For he gives his sunlight to both the evil and the good, and he sends rain on the just and the unjust alike. If you love only those who love you, what reward is there for that? Even corrupt tax collectors do that much. If you are kind only to your friends, how are you different from anyone else? Even pagans do that.

These aren't easy words, but we can't just ignore them—this is Jesus talking...

Яeverse

With all the high drama that surrounds the typical teenager, I feel pretty confident in assuming that there are probably some "difficult" people in your life that you just don't like very much. Yet Jesus' call to love those you don't even like stands before you like a stake in the ground. He's calling you to relate differently to them. Have a talk with God today about the difficult people in your life and ask Him to give you the kind of love He has.

Яemember

But God showed his great love for us by sending Christ to die for us while we were still sinners (Romans 5:8). Jesus' compassion for us compels us to have compassion for others—including the difficult people in our lives.

#6 A GOD IN HEAVEN

Яead
Daniel 2:25-28

Яecharge
Once ushered into the presence of King Nebuchadnezzar, it was time for Daniel to shine. This was his big moment, his time to polish his image, demonstrate his unparalleled skills and further enhance his cred with the king...maybe even ask for a raise (just joking).

But Daniel didn't puff himself up like a peacock or strut his stuff. When the king asked him, point blank, if he was able to interpret the troubling dream, Daniel was open, honest and humble about the source of the insights he was about to share. He told the king no **man** could explain his mysterious dream, *"BUT there is a God in heaven who reveals mysteries"* and holds the future.

Now, there's a spiritual conversation starter for you. Daniel deflected all attention away from himself and toward the one, true God and the mysteries that God had revealed to him. With this brief statement, Daniel set the stage to make the reality of God, and the message God had revealed to him, the focal point of the coming conversation.

Reflect

You, too, have the awesome opportunity to reveal the mysteries of God to others. Not in the "interpretation of a dream" like Daniel did, but in the message God has revealed to us through Jesus. When you share Jesus' message of grace and hope with your friends, you're unlocking the mysteries of God for them!

Reverse

God has specifically placed you in your own circle of influence, so you can reveal the mystery of the cross, and share with others the free gift of salvation that's available to anyone who trusts in Jesus.

In the halls, during lunch, after school, on the phone or wherever, actively look for ways to steer your conversations toward spiritual things today. Like Daniel, be totally open and honest with your friends about who God is in your life, and how the gospel changes everything for all eternity.

Remember

When you're sharing your faith with someone who believes differently than you about Jesus, try using the "ask, admire and admit" approach in your conversation.

- **Ask** them questions about what they believe, not to trap them, but to understand them and break down any relational barriers that are keeping them from considering Jesus.

- **Admire** everything you can about what they believe in order to help people open up. Find areas of common ground you can compliment them on. Even if you don't agree with their beliefs, you can always affirm their honesty.

- **Admit** that the reason you are a Christian is that you know you've fallen short and need someone to rescue you. That someone is Jesus.

As you **ask** honest questions, **admire** what you can about what others believe and **admit** your own need for Jesus, their guard will drop and you can begin to engage them in a real conversation about Jesus and the good news of the gospel.

Яenew

Dear God, as I look for opportunities today to steer my conversations toward You, please help me be open and honest with my friends about who You are in my life, so they can come to know You too. In Jesus' name, amen.

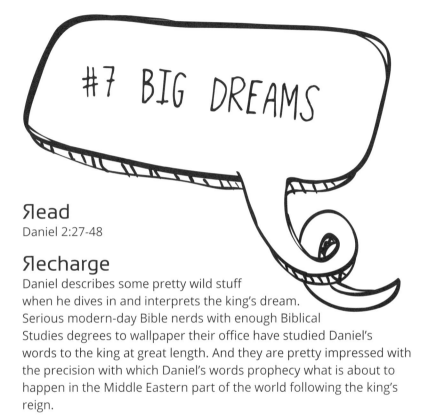

#7 BIG DREAMS

Яead
Daniel 2:27-48

Яecharge
Daniel describes some pretty wild stuff
when he dives in and interprets the king's dream.
Serious modern-day Bible nerds with enough Biblical
Studies degrees to wallpaper their office have studied Daniel's
words to the king at great length. And they are pretty impressed with
the precision with which Daniel's words prophecy what is about to
happen in the Middle Eastern part of the world following the king's
reign.

The overarching message of the dream was God's power and
authority over the rise and fall of kingdoms, both earthly and
heavenly. Through the dream, God laid out the coming progression
of kingdoms that would directly impact the nation of Israel.

The "Daniel for Dummies" version of the imagery in the dream goes
like this:

- The Neo-Babylonian Empire of King Nebuchadnezzar (represented by the head of gold)

- The Medo-Persian Empire (represented by silver)

- The Greek Empire established by Alexander the Great (represented by bronze)

- The Roman Empire (represented by iron)

- God's Coming Eternal Kingdom established by Jesus the Messiah (represented by the Rock that will be over "the whole earth" for all eternity), which will come into its full dominion at Christ's second coming.

Now you have to remember that when Daniel spoke these prophecies for the king, #1 was the only one that had happened, the rest are a foretelling of the future. And that's what makes it so amazing. It's when historians look back across the intervening centuries that the full meaning and impressive accuracy of Daniel's prophecies fall into place.

Reflect

Old Testament prophecies like those found in this passage of Daniel, help us in a couple different ways. First, they give us confidence in the divine inspiration of the Bible. Did you know that there are 300+ Old Testament prophecies about Jesus? These prophecies include everything from where He would be born to how He would die. The odds of these 300 prophecies being fulfilled by one person are 1 in 10 to the 17th power, that's 100,000,000,000,000,000, making Jesus' fulfillment of all of them truly astounding. (Source: Josh McDowell, *The New Evidence That Demands a Verdict*, p. 193). This clearly points to the divine inspiration of Scripture.

But secondly, the prophetic accuracy of passages like this one found in the book of Daniel also gives us confidence that no matter what earthly kingdom's rise and fall, God is in control of history. Whether the Middle East explodes in hostilities, Afghanistan erupts in chaos or North Korea launches a nuclear missile, the present, broken world order will not last forever.

The Bible assures us that in the fullness of time, Jesus will return and establish a kingdom that will last forever. And that, as followers of Christ, we will be part of His eternal kingdom. Pretty cool, huh?

Яeverse

Revelations 21:1-7 describes the Apostle John's vision of heaven.

Then I saw a new heaven and a new earth, for the old heaven and the old earth had disappeared. And the sea was also gone. And I saw the holy city, the new Jerusalem, coming down from God out of heaven like a bride beautifully dressed for her husband.

I heard a loud shout from the throne, saying, "Look, God's home is now among his people! He will live with them, and they will be his people. God himself will be with them. He will wipe every tear from their eyes, and there will be no more death or sorrow or crying or pain. All these things are gone forever."

And the one sitting on the throne said, "Look, I am making everything new!" And then he said to me, "Write this down, for what I tell you is trustworthy and true." And he also said, "It is finished! I am the Alpha and the Omega—the Beginning and the End. To all who are thirsty I will give freely from the springs of the water of life. All who are victorious will inherit all these blessings, and I will be their God, and they will be my children.

FINISH THIS SENTENCE.

GOD, THE THING I'M MOST LOOKING FORWARD TO ABOUT YOUR COMING ETERNAL KINGDOM IS...

_____

_____

_____

_____

_____

Яemember

Most people are intrigued by the whole idea of "Armageddon" and the end of the world. Ask one of your unreached friends what they think about the end of the world, and use the conversation as an opportunity to talk about Jesus' promise that He's coming back.

#8 IDOLS THEN AND NOW

Яead
Daniel 3:1-7

Яecharge

Clearly King Nebuchadnezzar had a thing about gold. Anyone who builds a **90 foot high** golden idol and demands that everyone bow down to worship it has some serious gold-love going on.

The real kicker for the Hebrews was that the king demanded their obedience to this decree or else they would be thrown into a blazing furnace.

We learn a few things about the king here.

- He was rich...that was a lot of gold.

- He was controlling...it was my way or the highway (the "hotway" might be another way to put it).

- He was powerful…he expected to be obeyed without question and was prepared to make the consequences for anyone who thought differently extremely painful.

- He was misguided…you only go to this kind of trouble if you think worshipping an idol like this is actually going to help you somehow.

Яeflect

In our day, we find it hard to believe that someone would create a golden idol like this one, and demand that others bow down to it, or else.

But if you look past the statue itself, down deeper into the essential nature of any kind of idolatry, is it really so different from what we do today?

We all too often listen and respond obediently when the rich, controlling, or powerful—however misguided—tell us that we should believe this, act like that, buy this, dress like that, or else… Many of us snap to attention whenever someone, some hot trend or some corporate brand is trying to get us to bow down to the newest must-have idol—the latest tech toy, the newest clothing style or the drive to be popular at all costs.

None of these "things" are necessarily bad in and of themselves, but whenever they become more important in your life than God is, that's idolatry.

Here's a concrete example, whether you want to call it an "idol" or not, just imagine what it would look like if you were as tuned in to God and His Word as you are to your cell phone.

IT'S TIME TO START THINKING DIFFERENTLY!

What kinds of things are vying for top priority in your life? Think about the ways these things sometimes pull you away from God.

- _____
- _____
- _____
- _____
- _____
- _____
- _____

The key here is not necessarily that you push these things down your priority list. It's that you give these things to God, and invite Jesus into them so that they become about Him and not about you. Think differently by putting God smack in the middle of them.

Яemember

Our tech toys don't have to be something that pull us away from God, if we use them well, they can enhance our walk with Him. For a great example of this, download the free Dare 2 Share mobile app at <u>dare2share.org/mobileapp</u> today. Watch the training and use the resources on the app to help you share the gospel.

Яenew

Dear God, I want to surrender these things that are pulling me away from You. Please help me plug into Your strength and Your power, so that moment-by-moment, I can live for Your glory.

Яead
Daniel 3:8-12

Яecharge
The stage was set. The golden idol was in place, and the king's decree to bow down and worship or face the fiery furnace was issued.

And then, in walked jealousy. The court astrologers quickly beat a path to the king's door so they could destroy their Jewish "competition." By way of background, here's a little more of the back story. Near the end of Daniel 2, after Daniel had successfully interpreted the king's dream, Scripture tells us:

Then the king appointed Daniel to a high position and gave him many valuable gifts. He made Daniel ruler over the whole province of Babylon, as well as chief over all his wise men. At Daniel's request, the king appointed Shadrach, Meshach, and Abednego to be in charge of all the affairs of the province of Babylon, while Daniel remained in the king's court (Daniel 2:48-49).

So here were these foreign-born young Jews who'd been elevated to a higher position in the king's court than the Babylonians. Is it any wonder they were hot to get Shadrach, Meshach and Abednego in trouble if they could?

There was no love lost when the court astrologers trotted in to the king and announced: *"There are some Jews—Shadrach, Meshach, and Abednego—whom you have put in charge of the province of Babylon. They pay no attention to you, Your Majesty. They refuse to serve your gods and do not worship the gold statue you have set up"* (Daniel 3:12).

Яeflect

The Biblical account of Shadrach, Meshach and Abednego and the fiery furnace never tells us why Daniel is not mentioned in these unfolding events. Perhaps he was away traveling on the king's business. Some believe he was back in Babylon taking care of the king's business while Neb was out in the countryside, demanding his subjects worship his image. Whatever the reason, it appears that he was not swept up in this life and death drama. But fortunately for these other three Hebrews, they were not facing this difficult time alone. They were in it together—they were what I like to call a "Cause Crew," a small group of close friends who are committed right alongside you to Christ and His Cause.

Did you know that it's a timeless truth of Scripture that you will be stronger in facing down your struggles and battles if you have others beside you? Ecclesiastes 4:12 puts it like this, *"A person standing alone can be attacked and defeated, but two can stand back-to-back and conquer. Three are even better, for a triple-braided cord is not easily broken."*

The Christian life wasn't meant to be lived in isolation. So think differently about the believers around you. Value them, encourage them, lean on them. We all need others to encourage us, challenge us and help us stand strong in our faith.

Яeverse

Do you have a few Christian friends you can turn to? If so, connect with them today, and ask them how you can be praying for them. If not, spend some time right now praying that God would help you find some friends to fill this hole.

Яemember

Consider Jesus' words: *"So now I am giving you a new commandment: Love each other. Just as I have loved you, you should love each other. Your love for one another will prove to the world that you are my disciples"* (John 13:34-35). When believers love and care for each other, what impact can it have on those who don't know Jesus?

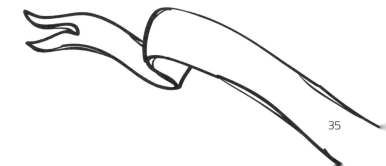

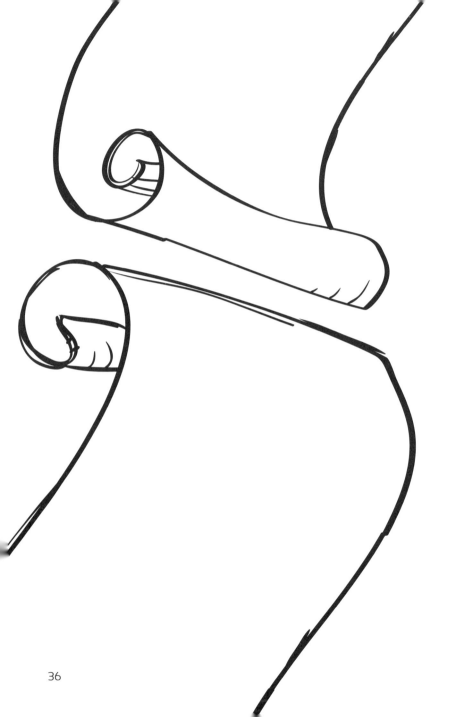

#10 A LETHAL LINE IN THE SAND

Яead
Daniel 3:13-15

Яecharge
ULTIMATUM TIME! Informed of Shadrach, Meshach, and Abednego's open defiance in refusing to bow down to the golden idol, the outraged king drew a line in the sand. *"I will give you one more chance to bow down and worship the statue."* If the three Hebrews dared disobey this direct order from the king, the fiery furnace awaited.

Babylon was a multi-theistic culture that believed in many gods. The king was simply demanding that these three do what everyone else did—worship another god. No big deal, right?

Wrong. For numero uno of the Ten Commandments was: *"You shall have no other gods before me. You shall not make for yourself an idol."*

And the king didn't just leave it at the level of an ultimatum to obey him. He added a mocking taunt: *"Then what god will be able to rescue you from my power?"* With that question, the confrontation escalated to an outright battle between the Hebrew God's power to rescue them vs. the king's power to destroy them.

Яeflect

Every day, you too are being pushed and prodded to embrace behaviors that dishonor God and prompt you to question His centrality in your life.

Whether they're big things or small, you too face the pull to compromise. An invitation to gossip here...an opportunity to cheat there...an inappropriate picture to look at...a lie to get you out of trouble...

On and on the lines in the sand stretch out before you, prompting you to disregard God's call to a holy life and tempting you to dismiss the Holy Spirit's moment-by-moment guidance in the choices you face every day. Do you bow down and surrender to the temptations? Or do you lean into God's power to rescue you?

Don't succumb to sin's power to discourage and destroy. Think differently. Put on the full armor of God that equips you to stand firm. Instead of seeing sin as an alluring temptation, see it as it is—a deceptive distraction that weakens your character, calluses your soul and damages your relationship with God.

Яeverse

Confess to God for the times you've missed the mark in the past. Then pray through the following powerful passage about the armor of God and ask Him to help you step up and start thinking differently.

Get serious about tapping into God's power, as you confront the temptations in your life that dishonor God.

Therefore, put on every piece of God's armor so you will be able to resist the enemy in the time of evil. Then after the battle you will still be standing firm. Stand your ground, putting on the belt of truth and the body armor of God's righteousness. For shoes, put on the peace that comes from the Good News so that you will be fully prepared. In addition to all of these, hold up the shield of faith to stop the fiery arrows of the devil. Put on salvation as your helmet, and take the sword of the Spirit, which is the word of God.

Pray in the Spirit at all times and on every occasion. Stay alert and be persistent in your prayers for all believers everywhere (Ephesians 6:13-18).

Яemember

The same power that saved us from the penalty of sin saves us from the power of sin. You have unreached friends who need to hear about God's amazing power. Share the website www.LifeIn6Words.com with one friend who needs Jesus today.

#11 HOW TO GROW A BACKBONE

Яead
Daniel 3:16-18

Яecharge
With the king's taunting ultimatum ringing in their ears, Shadrach, Meshach, and Abednego stepped up to the challenge. Drawing upon their faith in God and His power to rescue, they countered with a bold, gutsy response.

Their words were firm without being cocky, and exuded total faith that God was in control no matter the outcome for them personally. *"If we are thrown into the blazing furnace, the God whom we serve is able to save us. He will rescue us from your power, Your Majesty. But even if he doesn't, we want to make it clear to you, Your Majesty, that we will never serve your gods or worship the gold statue you have set up"* (Daniel 3:17-18).

Not a single, quivering doubt about it: they would not compromise their loyalty to the one, true God and they would willingly pay with their lives, if it came to that.

Яeflect

Backbone. Guts. Courage. Where **do** they come from? How **do** you grow a spiritual backbone like that?

There's a one word answer: faith. You only grow this kind of backbone by leaning into your faith relationship with Jesus day in and day out. As you move deeper and deeper into a living, vibrant, give-and-take relationship with Him, you'll grow more and more confident in the immensity of His love, the reach of His sovereignty and the depth of His goodness. It's this kind of growing relationship with Him that builds your spiritual backbone, so that you increasingly trust Him in all things. Even knowing that, having faith doesn't always mean we'll be spared from difficulty.

This kind of faith doesn't just drop into your lap fully bloomed. It's kind of like working out. In the same way that your muscles develop through running or through reps at the gym, your "faith muscles" also develop with use. As you exercise faith in small things, like seeking God's direction in the midst of life choices, you'll find your faith being honed and toned.

We see an example of this with Daniel and his friends in Daniel 1:8-16, when they stood firm and didn't compromise in the small area of God's dietary rules for them. These small acts of faith served as the practice ground for the tougher times ahead that would call for immense faith.

So, start by standing firm and trusting God in the small things, and you'll find yourself growing a spiritual backbone that will carry you through the tough stuff.

Яeverse

Think of one area of your life right now where you need to lean on God more. It could be anything: something painful you're trying to deal with, a sin area of struggle or your timidity about talking to others about Jesus, to name a few.

Pray that God will help you begin to think differently about this area. Begin to exercise more faith in Him as you wrestle with it. To help you start thinking differently, do a Google® search of Bible verses that deal with the issue and spend time in these verses. Choose the verse that fits you best, and memorize it. It will help you begin to grow your spiritual backbone.

Яemember

Approach a non-Christian friend today who is going through a hard time, and ask them if there's anything you can do for them. Look for an opportunity to tell them about how you're learning to lean on God in the midst of tough stuff of your life. Ask if you can pray for them.

43

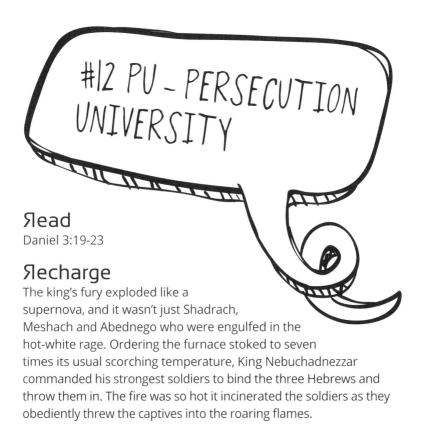

#12 PU – PERSECUTION UNIVERSITY

Яead
Daniel 3:19-23

Яecharge
The king's fury exploded like a supernova, and it wasn't just Shadrach, Meshach and Abednego who were engulfed in the hot-white rage. Ordering the furnace stoked to seven times its usual scorching temperature, King Nebuchadnezzar commanded his strongest soldiers to bind the three Hebrews and throw them in. The fire was so hot it incinerated the soldiers as they obediently threw the captives into the roaring flames.

Why was the king so outraged? Because he was powerful, controlling and accustomed to being obeyed without question. I'm guessing he was even used to his subjects cowering at his feet and begging for his mercy. Now these three bold, brave, principled Hebrews were standing up to him, challenging his ego-centric view of himself and his misguided beliefs about how the world works.

Яeflect
Sometimes, when you exercise your spiritual backbone by taking a stand for your faith or sharing the message of the gospel, you too

may encounter negative reactions. While you may not be physically persecuted like the trio in Daniel, even the eye rolling or cold shoulder you get can feel like fiery flames.

The even harsher reality is that there may be times when your faith triggers undeserved and unreserved hostility. Whenever you nudge people toward Biblical truth, there's a possibility they will lash out in response. Their hostile reaction could spring from some hurt they've experienced in the past at the hands of judgmental Christians, or they could be angry at God, and taking it out on you. Or like King Nebuchadnezzar, it could be that they are ego-centric, misguided or stubbornly unwilling to acknowledge the reality of God.

So you may encounter rejection, taunting or worse from friends and enemies alike. I call this PU—Persecution University. Daniel and his friends went through Persecution U. So did Jesus, Paul, Peter and every single one of Christ's original apostles.

Яeverse

Have you ever found yourself enrolled in PU? If so, take strength from Jesus' words below in Matthew 5:10-12 which challenge you to think differently. If you haven't walked this road yet, it's likely only a matter of time before you will, so get yourself prepared.

> *"God blesses those who are persecuted for doing right, for the Kingdom of Heaven is theirs. God blesses you when people mock you and persecute you and lie about you and say all sorts of evil things against you because you are my followers. Be happy about it! Be very glad! For a great reward awaits you in heaven. And remember, the ancient prophets were persecuted in the same way"* (Matthew 5:10-12).

Have an honest conversation with God about what you are willing to suffer or sacrifice for His sake.

DEAR JESUS,

You suffered for me on the cross, so it's out of gratitude for Your great gift of my salvation that I want to serve You with everything I am. I want to start thinking differently about being "persecuted" for Your sake, so I give You my friendships, my popularity, my image, my....

_____

_____

_____

_____

_____

_____

_____

_____

_____

_____

_____

Яemember

As you share your faith with others, you may encounter some people who are openly hostile to Jesus and Christianity. Remember that having other Christians around you will help you during the times you face persecution for your faith.

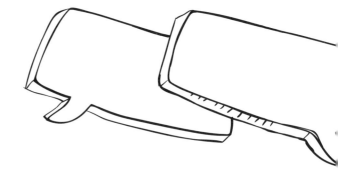

#13 RESCUE!

Яead
Daniel 3:24-27

Яecharge

Miraculously, God came to the rescue! Inside the fiery furnace, Shadrach, Meshach, and Abednego were seen walking about—unbound, unscorched, unharmed. And unalone! For with them, in the midst of the flames, a fourth man appeared—someone King Nebuchadnezzar described as looking *"like a god."* Shouting in amazement, the king commanded that the Hebrews come out of the fire. And out the three came, without even the smell of smoke on their clothing.

The book of Daniel never tells us exactly who the "fourth man" in the furnace was. We know only that he supernaturally showed up during their trial by fire and that he looked *"like a god."* He could have been an angel or a preincarnate appearance of Christ (a physical manifestation of Christ before he was born into the world in Bethlehem). But regardless of who this supernatural being was, Shadrach, Meshach, and Abednego's courageous, unflinching faithfulness was rewarded. They'd stood firm in their faith, and God came to their rescue.

Яeflect

These young men's steely bravery and God's miraculous intervention in the face of **serious** trouble should send a chill down your spine.

But does having faith mean that we will always be supernaturally rescued from our troubles? No. When you think about it, even this trio of great faith eventually died...so, no, even people like these three who had unyielding confidence in God hit the place where physical death finally arrived.

The message of this story is not that God will always ride to the rescue supernaturally. Rather, the timeless truth here is that come what may, no matter how dark things look, we're called to walk by faith and then leave the results to God, knowing that nothing (including death) can ever separate us from His love. Check out this awe-inspiringly amazing passage written to you:

> And I am convinced that nothing can ever separate us from God's love. Neither death nor life, neither angels nor demons, neither our fears for today nor our worries about tomorrow—not even the powers of hell can separate us from God's love. No power in the sky above or in the earth below—indeed, nothing in all creation will ever be able to separate us from the love of God that is revealed in Christ Jesus our Lord (Romans 8:38-39).

Яeverse

Read the above passage in Romans again and this time circle every single thing that God promises cannot come between you and His love. Tell God thank you.

Яemember

You have friends who are missing out on the immense love of God. Copy the most famous verse in the Bible: *"For God loved the world so much that he gave his one and only Son, so that everyone who believes in him will not perish but have eternal life"* (John 3:16). Text it, email it, post it or give it to a friend who needs Jesus today, and ask them what they think it means. Open up the dialogue, and get the conversation started about Jesus and His message of grace.

Яenew

Dear God, thank You that no matter how tough things might get in my life, I can trust that You will always be there with me, because You've told me in Your Word that nothing can ever separate me from Your love. Help me share Your message of love with those around me, through both my words and my deeds. In Jesus' name, amen.

Яead
Daniel 3:28-30

Яecharge
Nebuchadnezzar was immensely wowed by the Hebrew God's power to rescue Shadrach, Meshach and Adednego. So impressed, in fact, that he issued an order declaring that anyone who spoke a word against this powerful God would be *"torn limb from limb"*! Not to mention that his deconstruction crews would make quick work of leveling the humble abodes of any bad-mouthers. Sort of sounds like he'd fit right in with the mafia...

But still, ya gotta love the guy's sudden enthusiasm for defending the reputation of the almighty God of the Universe.

Now things had come full circle. With these vividly graphic decrees from the king, the envious "wise men" who had started this whole life and death drama in the first place were put on notice—along with everyone else: Don't disrespect this God. The king was so impressed with this Jewish trio, that he promoted them to even higher positions in his government.

Яeflect

Don't you love it when someone first starts to get a glimpse of how amazing God is? They can express it in some of the most inappropriate ways!

When I was a pastor, our church routinely saw tons of rough, tough people coming to Christ each year. Thanks to these enthusiastic newbies who didn't know much about "Christian" ways yet, it was not unusual to hear f-bombs going off in the church lobby, as they were describing how awesome Jesus is. Their unvarnished, unbridled, overflowing enthusiasm for Jesus was on full, though inappropriate, display.

You see a bit of this same phenomenon happening here with King Nebuchadnezzar. As the king started learning more about the Hebrews' God, he developed a growing respect—which for him, translated into full-scale threats to his subjects if they dared speak against this powerful God.

Яeverse

You too can help your friends develop a growing respect for the one, true God as you tell them more and more about Him through both your words and your deeds. Of course, it's never appropriate to threaten or coerce others like we saw the king doing, but with a little gentle, loving effort, it's not difficult to turn an everyday conversation toward spiritual things.

Be open and honest with a friend today about how God has rescued you!

Яemember
Check out the video "Have You Ever Wondered About God?" at
<u>somethingamazing.net/GOD</u>. Send the video to an unreached friend
and then use it as conversation starter to talk about Jesus.

Яenew
Dear God, You are so amazing that I want to tell everyone about how
incredible You are! Help me bravely launch into real, give-and-take
spiritual conversations about You with my friends today. In Jesus'
name, amen.

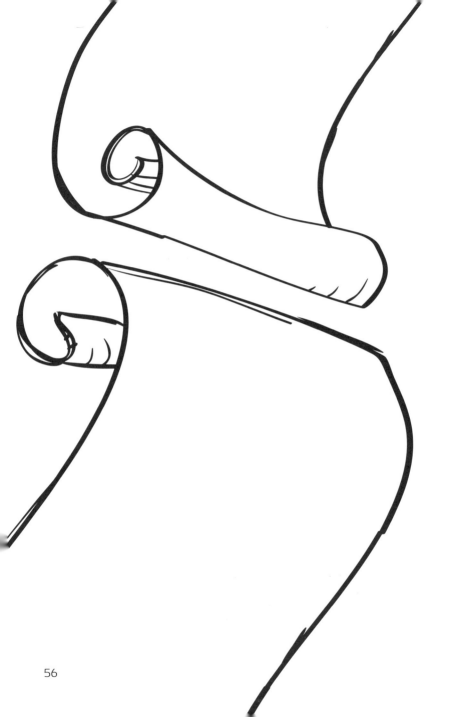

#15 PURSUE EXCELLENCE

Яead
Daniel 6:1-3

Яecharge
Years passed. Kings rose and fell. We pick up Daniel's story again in Daniel 6.

In the intervening years, the kingdom of Babylon had been conquered by the Persians, and now there was a new king on the throne, Darius the Mede. As the new king grabbed the reins of power, he divided up his kingdom into 120 provinces (states). He appointed a governor to rule each geographic area. Over these 120 governors he placed Daniel and two other high officials, tasking them with administering his kingdom and protecting his interests.

Once again, Daniel's excellent ability made him stand out in the new king's eyes. And because of Daniel's superior service, the king made plans to move him into the topmost supervisory slot as COO (chief operating officer) over the entire empire. Quite a stellar promotion!

This was an amazing career path for someone who had originally started out years before as a teenage captive hauled away in bondage to Babylon.

Яeflect

What accounts for this stellar trajectory?

Clear back in Daniel 1, when Daniel and his three Hebrew friends were still fresh new teenage recruits in the king's court, you see the groundwork for excellence being laid:

> *God gave these four young men an unusual aptitude for understanding every aspect of literature and wisdom...The king talked with them, and no one impressed him as much...So they entered the royal service. Whenever the king consulted them in any matter requiring wisdom and balanced judgment, he found them ten times more capable than any of the magicians and enchanters in his entire kingdom,* (Daniel 1: 17, 19-20).

These young men started out pursuing excellence while they were students in training. It was simply part of who they were as followers of the one, true God. They knew that being effective, influential representatives of God in the place He had put them demanded excellence.

The same is true for you. God has planted you where you are and given you a purpose: to be His ambassador. Consider this snapshot of God's mission for you as His follower:

God has given us this task of reconciling people to him. For God was in Christ, reconciling the world to himself, no longer counting people's sins against them. And he gave us this wonderful message of reconciliation. So we are Christ's ambassadors; God is making his appeal through us. We speak for Christ when we plead, "Come back to God!" (2 Corinthians 5:18-20).

Strive to be the best you can be in everything you do, in order that you might be an effective, compelling ambassador for Him in your sphere of influence. When you pursue excellence for the sake of God's glory, it's an act of worship!

Яeverse
Consider this statement: Work like it all depends upon you, and pray like it all depends upon God.

Share this statement with one or both of your parents today. Ask them what they think of it.

Яemember
As Christ's ambassador, it's important to know how to share your faith with excellence. Go back to page 12 (devo #3) and re-read the GOSPEL box. If you need to review the GOSPEL acrostic, spend some time getting familiar with it so you can explain Jesus' message to others in a clear and compelling way.

WRITE IT OUT BELOW

_____

_____

_____

_____

_____

_____

_____

_____

_____

For more help learning how to share your faith effectively, pick up a copy of the *Dare 2 Share: A Field Guide to Sharing Your Faith* at dare2share.org/store.

Яenew

Dear God, what an amazing privilege to be Your ambassador. Please help me pursue excellence in all I do and represent You to the very best of my ability. I want to worship You in all I say and do. In Jesus' name, amen.

#16 LIVE WITH INTEGRITY

Яead
Daniel 6:4

Яecharge
Some dark truths about human nature are timeless. And here's one such unfortunate reality: Jealousy is always waiting in the wings for a chance to break loose and wreak havoc.

So even though years had passed, and there was a new king on the block, once again we find the other high officers of the king's court green with envy about Daniel's imminent promotion to top dog. These officials were desperately looking for anything that might derail Daniel's rise to power over them.

But they were stumped. Try as they might to find some evidence of incompetence or corruption, they came up empty-handed. Daniel was *"faithful, always responsible, and completely trustworthy."* He was a model of integrity in all dimensions of his life. Beyond reproach. No wonder these conniving, corrupt charlatans had it out for him.

Яeflect

Faithful. Responsible. Trustworthy.

Do these words describe you? Are you putting on the character of Christ each day and living a life of integrity? Is your word, your word? Are you worthy of trust?

Check out the Apostle Paul's description of what a life of integrity in Christ looks like:

> *Since you have heard about Jesus and have learned the truth that comes from him, throw off your old sinful nature and your former way of life, which is corrupted by lust and deception. Instead, let the Spirit renew your thoughts and attitudes. Put on your new nature, created to be like God—truly righteous and holy.*
>
> *So stop telling lies...And don't sin by letting anger control you...If you are a thief, quit stealing. Instead, use your hands for good hard work, and then give generously to others in need. Don't use foul or abusive language. Let everything you say be good and helpful, so that your words will be an encouragement to those who hear them. And do not bring sorrow to God's Holy Spirit by the way you live. Remember, he has identified you as his own, guaranteeing that you will be saved on the day of redemption. Get rid of all bitterness, rage, anger, harsh words, and slander, as well as all types of evil behavior* (Ephesians 4:21-31).

How are you doing?

When you get up and start each day, choose to act with integrity. Much like you choose daily what to wear or what to eat, consciously choose to let the Spirit renew your thoughts and then actively put on the new you in Christ.

Яeverse

Pick one sin area you struggle with. Lying, gossip, porn, lust, cheating...or whatever. Pray and ask God to help you change your behavior, and help you grow into a person of integrity in this area. Choose daily to live with integrity. Don't just beat yourself up about this sin, instead, refocus on God whenever temptation rears its ugly head. Follow the advice in Philippians 4:8: *"And now, dear brothers and sisters, one final thing. Fix your thoughts on what is true, and honorable, and right, and pure, and lovely, and admirable. Think about things that are excellent and worthy of praise."*

Enlist one trustworthy friend to hold you accountable, as you strive to let the Holy Spirit have total control of this area of your life.

Яemember

Whether you know it or not, your non-Christian friends are quietly watching you to see if you're a Christian who is walking in integrity or hypocrisy. This doesn't mean you have to be perfect, because that's impossible. Just be quick to acknowledge your faults and failings and then pick yourself up and strive to do better as Jesus' ambassador.

64

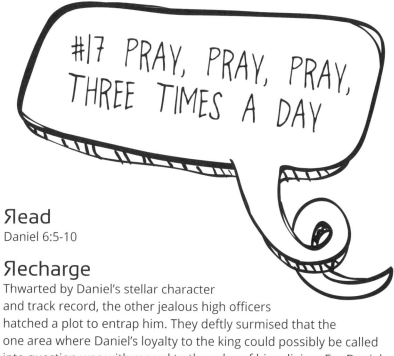

#17 PRAY, PRAY, PRAY, THREE TIMES A DAY

Яead
Daniel 6:5-10

Яecharge
Thwarted by Daniel's stellar character and track record, the other jealous high officers hatched a plot to entrap him. They deftly surmised that the one area where Daniel's loyalty to the king could possibly be called into question was with regard to the rules of his religion. For Daniel was known to faithfully pray to his one, true God. So these devious officials maneuvered the king into signing a strict decree that any person who prayed to anyone other than the king himself would be thrown into the lions' den.

When Daniel learned about the new law, he was unfazed. With calm, steely determination, he went home, knelt down near an open window for all the world to see and prayed three times a day just as he had always done.

Яeflect

Why pray three times a day? It's not really the number that's important. But touching base with God at multiple points throughout your day is a great help in keeping your focus on God in everything you're about.

What does a healthy prayer life look like? Of course, it looks different for different people, but Jesus provides a model for us. When His followers came to Him and asked Him to teach them how to pray, He gave them the Lord's Prayer.

Яeverse

Because it makes it easy to remember, I like to break out the Lord's Prayer into four distinct parts, which spell out the acrostic PRAY. Personalize your prayer below, using Jesus' model. Then try actually kneeling down and lifting these requests up to God three times a day so you can cultivate the habit of inviting God into your day, all day long.

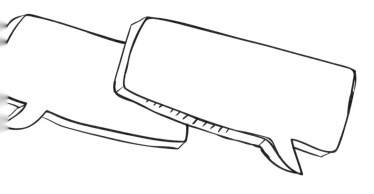

PRAISE *"Our Father in heaven, hallowed by thy Name."*
Connect intimately with God as your Daddy.

Dear God,

_____

_____

_____

REQUEST *"Thy kingdom come, Thy will be done on earth, as it is in heaven. Give us this day our daily bread."*
Pray for God's purposes to be accomplished on earth, like your friends who need Jesus coming to know Him. This is also where you ask God for your daily needs, including things like wisdom and strength.

_____

_____

_____

ADMIT

"And forgive us our debts, as we forgive our debtors." Ask God to clean the slate and give you a fresh start. This is a reset button to flush away the junk that's blocking your relationship with God and to help you get energized by His power and presence again.

_____

_____

_____

YIELD

"And lead us not into temptation, but deliver us from evil: For thine is the kingdom, and the power, and the glory, for ever. Amen." Ask God to lead you, not into temptation, but to advance His kingdom and power and glory forever.

_____

_____

_____

_____

Яemember

As you seek to see His "kingdom come," remember to pray for your friends who don't know Jesus yet.

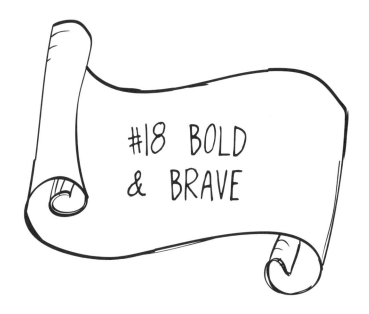

#18 BOLD
& BRAVE

Яead
Daniel 6:11-13

Яecharge
The malicious high officials went looking to see if they could get Daniel in trouble, based on this new decree. Once they confirmed that Daniel was still praying to the one, true God, they returned to the king. They prodded him to once again publically reaffirm the law's harsh, mandatory sentence and maneuvered him to acknowledge that no one could change the punishment for violators, including the king himself.

Then they sprang the trap, reporting that Daniel was disobeying the law and praying to God three times a day.

Яeflect

Daniel's deep, personal relationship with God superseded everything else. He was boldly, bravely and publicly committed to that relationship, even if it could cost him his very life. Why? Because he knew without a shadow of a doubt that life apart from his connection with God was worse than no life at all.

Imagine taking your connection with God so seriously that you would rather die than hide it from the world around you. What would it look like if your relationship with Jesus was on full display, regardless of the fallout that might come in terms of your coolness factor? Vibrantly, publicly living out his faith was an absolute, daily essential for Daniel—no matter what. Is it for you?

Яeverse

Gather your courage and think of one thing you can do today that will publically display your commitment to Jesus, not in a flaunting, showy way, but in a brave, quietly determined way. It could be sheltering someone else from a bully or a gossip, walking away from a cheating opportunity, wearing a Christian t-shirt, bravely redirecting a conversation toward Jesus, praying before you eat your food in the school cafeteria or actively sharing your faith with a friend. Prayerfully decide on a course of action. Then do it!

Яemember

So never be ashamed to tell others about our Lord. And don't be ashamed of me, either, even though I'm in prison for him. With the strength God gives you, be ready to suffer with me for the sake of the Good News (2 Timothy 1:8).

Яenew

Dear God, I want to declare to You right now that I am not ashamed to tell others about You. Through Your strength and for Your glory, help me publicly display my faith in You today—not to be flaunting or showy—but rather to be loving and engaging. In Jesus' name, amen.

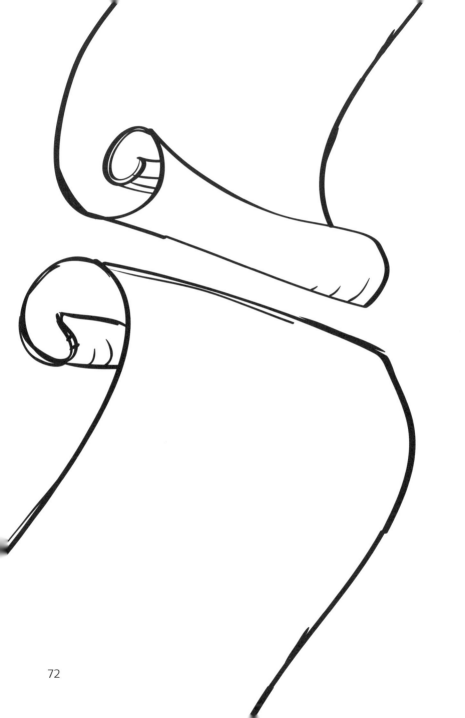

#19 FACING THE DARKEST NIGHT

Яead
Daniel 6:14-20

Яecharge

King Darius was distressed as the trap to destroy Daniel sprang shut. Because the king highly valued this excellent, trustworthy servant, he racked his brains for a solution to this deadly dilemma. But he could not backpedal on his decree, and was therefore powerless to rescue Daniel from the mandatory sentence of death-by-lion.

Reluctantly, the king issued the edict that cast Daniel into the lions' den and sealed the stone. No human would be riding in to rescue him. Even the king acknowledged that Daniel's only remaining hope was that the God he served would rescue him.

73

After an anguished, sleepless night, the king rushed to the lions' den in the morning calling, *"Daniel, servant of the living God! Was your God, whom you serve so faithfully, able to rescue you from the lions?"*

It's clear that even though the king wasn't a believer in the one, true God himself, he'd been wondering, watching and hoping against all odds that in Daniel's darkest hour, God had come to the rescue.

Яeflect

Have you ever considered that the way you cling to God through the trials and tough stuff of life may be one of the most powerful witnesses you can live out before your unreached friends?

Your hope in God need never, ever waver, for He has promised His followers: *"I will never fail you. I will never abandon you"* (Hebrews 13:5). This doesn't mean we will never have troubles in this life. On the contrary, Jesus actually told us to expect them in John 16:33: *"Here on earth you will have many trials and sorrows. But take heart, because I have overcome the world."* But when life gets dark and difficult, the loving presence of Christ and the hope of heaven provide comfort beyond words.

When you're walking through trials, the courage and comfort you draw from your faith in God provides the world with a vivid picture of the practical difference Jesus actually makes in your life. Is that hope shining in your life, in both word and attitude, for all those around you to see?

Яeverse

Is there something you're anxious about today? Mentally wrap it up in a bundle and place it at Jesus' feet. After you drop it there, ask Him to help you with it.

Яemember

Then Jesus said, "Come to me, all of you who are weary and carry heavy burdens, and I will give you rest. Take my yoke upon you. Let me teach you, because I am humble and gentle at heart, and you will find rest for your souls (Matthew 11:28-29).

Look for an opportunity to share the gospel with a friend today who is weary from carrying heavy burdens. They need to experience the hope found in Jesus.

75

#20 TOTAL TRUST

Яead
Daniel 6:21-24

Яecharge
No cliffhanger here...you very likely already know the rest of the story. Daniel survived the night in the lion's lair. King Darius was delighted that Daniel was alive, and ordered that he be lifted out of the lions' den. In retribution, the king further ordered that the malicious group who had masterminded this distressing episode be thrown to the lions instead.

But while the outcome of this story may be familiar to you, let's take a closer look at how Daniel described what was actually happening in the spiritual realm while he was in the lions' lair: " *'God sent an angel to shut the lions' mouths'...Not a scratch was found on him, for he had trusted in his God.*"

We can draw a couple important conclusions from this simple summary of what happened in the midst of Daniel's dark night:

- It was ultimately a spiritual battle.
- Daniel's total trust in God impacted the outcome.

Яeflect

Have you ever questioned whether God is really trustworthy? No matter what's coming down?

I get it, I really do. Sometimes it's really difficult to totally trust God, because we don't understand what He's up to, and how He could take something bad that's happening and possibly use it for good. But I find that it helps to think about it this way: We are on a need-to-know basis when it comes to God's larger plans and purposes.

Sometimes, things don't make sense to us because we can't see the big picture. But like a general in the midst of battle, God has a plan that He's unfolding, both for our good and for the good of His kingdom purposes. And we are His soldiers, called to follow our general. Sometimes there will be victories and sometimes defeats. Sometimes there will be a supernatural rescue, and sometimes not. But in all circumstances, we can trust God and His ability to work all things for good in our life (Romans 8:28) and in His larger plan for His kingdom to come and His will to be done here on earth as it is in heaven.

Яeverse

Trust in the Lord with all your heart;
do not depend on your own understanding.
Seek his will in all you do,
and he will show you which path to take (Proverbs 3:5-6).

Talk to God about these verses. Are you trusting Him or depending on your own strategies and plans? Are you seeking to do His will in everything you are about?

DEAR GOD,

WHEN I READ THIS PASSAGE IT MAKES ME REALIZE...

Яemember

As you seek to reach your unbelieving friends with the message of the gospel, and bring them to a place of trusting in Jesus, remember that ultimately you are involved in a spiritual battle for their souls.

We reject all shameful deeds and underhanded methods. We don't try to trick anyone or distort the word of God. We tell the truth before God, and all who are honest know this. If the Good News we preach is hidden behind a veil, it is hidden only from people who are perishing. Satan, who is the god of this world, has blinded the minds of those who don't believe. They are unable to see the glorious light of the Good News. They don't understand this message about the glory of Christ, who is the exact likeness of God (2 Corinthians 4:2-4).

#21 THE GOD WHO RESCUES

Яead
Daniel 6:25-28

Яecharge
King Darius had a long reach. When he spoke, people listened. With the snap of his fingers, people died, or were set free. Which makes it pretty, stinking incredible to think about how he proclaimed the truth about Daniel's God to his entire kingdom!

It's kinda like he pulled out his metaphorical mobile phone and sent out a mass text message proclaiming the awesome power of the one, true God! Check out the king's exact words in Daniel 6:26-27:

> *"I decree that everyone throughout my kingdom should tremble with fear before the God of Daniel.*
>
> *For he is the living God,*
> *and he will endure forever.*

His kingdom will never be destroyed,
and his rule will never end.
He rescues and saves his people;
he performs miraculous signs and wonders
in the heavens and on earth.
He has rescued Daniel
from the power of the lions."

Яeflect

Of course, there's one very critical thing wrong with the king's decree. Can you spot it?

You simply can't order people to acknowledge the one, true God as their God. It just doesn't work like that, even if you're a powerful king.

Why? Because God has designed the world, so that humans have this thing called choice. It is choice that allows each of us to make our own independent decision about whether we believe in God, and whether we choose to put our faith and trust in Him to rescue us and save us. That is at the core of Jesus' message in John 3:16-18:

> *"For God loved the world so much that he gave his one and only Son, so that everyone who believes in him will not perish but have eternal life. God sent his Son into the world not to judge the world, but to save the world through him. There is no judgment against anyone who believes in him. But anyone who does not believe in him has already been judged for not believing in God's one and only Son."*

Each person must make their own decision about whether they choose to believe in the God of the Bible or not. No one can decide for them, or force them into a saving faith.

82

Яeverse

King Darius was spot-on with a lot of what he had to say about Daniel's God. Take another look at Daniel 6:26-27 in the Яecharge section above. Circle the words in the passage that declare the following truths about God:

God is:
- living
- eternal
- indestructible
- ruler
- rescuer
- savior
- miracle worker

Just as Daniel's life and words helped the king begin to understand these truths about God, as Christ's ambassador, you've been called to that very same role of helping others know God and make Him known. Find a way to communicate the truth about God as rescuer to a friend who needs Jesus today by sharing a personal experience, a verse, a video, a letter, a book, a website, a text, a poem, or whatever other creative vehicle you want to use.

Яemember

Check out the gospel video at somethingamazing.net and use it to share your faith.

Яenew

DEAR GOD,

I PRAY FOR MY FRIEND, _____,
WHO DOESN'T KNOW YOU AS THEIR
RESCUER. I'M BEGGING YOU RIGHT NOW
THAT THEIR SPIRITUAL EYES WOULD BE
OPENED, AND THEY WOULD COME TO
SEE THE TRUTH OF JESUS' MESSAGE.
HELP ME COMMUNICATE THE GOSPEL IN
A CLEAR, COMPELLING WAY. IN JESUS'
NAME, AMEN.

DARE 2 SHARE

A Field Guide to Sharing Your Faith

by Greg Stier

This book serves as a ready reference for relationally sharing your faith. Throw it in your backpack for easy access to the invaluable faith-sharing tips and tools you'll find in this practical, real world resource. Features profiles on various belief systems, including compliments and conversation starters that will help you open up honest, authentic spiritual dialogue.

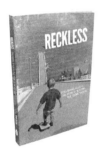

RECKLESS

Following Jesus to the Point of No Return

by Zane Black

Zane's casual style draws you in as he explores what being a fully committed Jesus follower looks like. He'll challenge you to personally and practically respond to Jesus' invitation to *"Come, follow me...and I will make you fishers of men."*

FIRESTARTER

by Greg Stier with Jane Dratz

Jared is an atheist with an attitude. Kailey is a new believer with a temper. See what can happen when just one teen takes on THE Cause of Christ at their high school. Learn tips and strategies that can help you make disciples who make disciples at your own school.

These and other great resources available at www.dare2share.org

MORE FROM DARE 2 SHARE

D2S ON YOUR PHONE

This mobile app will help train and inspire you to share your faith with your friends wherever you go! Go to dare2share.org/mobileapp to download the FREE Dare 2 Share app.

HOW TO SHARE YOUR FAITH WITH...

Have friends who are atheists? Agnostics? Into Wicca? The Dare 2 Share website features thirteen predominate worldviews for insights and questions that will help you engage your friends in a real conversation about Jesus and the good news of the gospel. Visit dare2share.org/worldviews

Hari the Hindu

Jenna the Jew

Jordan the Jehovah's Witness

Malik the Muslim

DARE 2 SHARE CONFERENCES

Join us at Dare 2 Share's weekend student evangelism training conferences, as well as youth leader training events. Current events schedule available at dare2share.org/events